KidCaps Presents

The Cold War:

A History Just for Kids

KidCaps is An Imprint of BookCaps™

www.bookcaps.com

Table of Contents

About KidCaps

KidCaps is an imprint of BookCaps™ that is just for kids! Each month BookCaps will be releasing several books in this exciting imprint. Visit are website or like us on Facebook to see more!

The flags of the United States and of the USSR, the two
main participants in the Cold War[1]

---

[1]   Image   source: http://blog.usni.org/wp-content/uploads/2010/04/Cold-War-Flags.jpg

Introduction

Have you ever been scared, worried that something awful was about to happen to you? Like when you hear a noise in the middle of the night and think that someone is trying to break into your house, or when you are lying in the dentist's chair, and you're scared that the procedure might really hurt? That feeling of worrying about something terrible that may happen is called "stress". Normally, feelings of stress don't last too long and are over rather quickly. But during the Cold War, which began in 1947 and lasted for over 40 years, millions of people lived each and every day worrying about what bad thing might happen to them; in other words, there was a lot of stress.

Have you ever heard of a Cold War? It sounds kind of strange, doesn't it? After all, when we talk about wars, we don't normally use the words "cold" and "hot" to describe them. We normally talk about how many soldiers died, how many bombs were dropped, or how much money a particular war cost. But in 1947, a special type of war began to be fought, one where the two nations fighting it never actually fired a bullet at each other or dropped a single bomb on each other's cities. It was a war of words, of secret agents, and of political tactics. Because there was no traditional fighting between the two sides, it was called a "Cold War".

The two main participants in this Cold War were the United States of America (USA) and the Union of Soviet Socialist Republics (USSR). For over 40 years, these two superpowers wrestled and made secret plans to make sure that the other one didn't get too strong. There were times when the Cold War looked like it was about to heat up and explode, and there were other times when it looked like the leaders were close to making peace.

During the terms of 9 US presidents and 4 representative leaders of the USSR, this war was fought. Millions of people were born and grew up under the shadow of this war, and many of them were afraid that the whole world would get involved and end up causing a third world war.

In this handbook, we will be learning more about the Cold War, and we will talk what were the things that motivated the two countries to compete with each other for over 40 years. You will find sections in here that divide up our study of the Cold War into six different main ideas.

The first section will talk about what led up to the Cold War. We will have a look at how the USSR was formed and what factors influenced the way its people looked at the United States. We will see how the USSR and the USA were allies during World War Two, but how all of that changed once the last shot of the war was fired.

The next section will focus on the "why", as in, "why did the Cold War happen"? Why did the two countries start to view each other as enemies and what were their motivations for trying to stop the other side from getting stronger? Politics are complicated, but in this section we will do our best to understand the reasons and thinking that influenced the decisions of everyone involved.

Then we will find out what actually happened during the Cold War. We will look at four different tools that each side used to try to make themselves stronger and the other guy weaker. The four tactics included:

- **Fighting proxy wars**
- **Spreading propaganda**
- **The space race**
- **Espionage**

You will get a first row seat to see how each of these methods worked and how they influenced daily life in each of the countries involved.

Then we will see what it was like to be a kid back then. What do you think it was like to grow up knowing that a huge country out there wanted to destroy the place where you lived? How would it feel to know that someone was spreading lies about you and your family to win an election or to score a political point? Would you have felt safe knowing that there were thousands of missiles aimed at your country, ready to be fired at a moment's notice?

The next section will show us how the Cold War finally came to an end. You may be surprised to find out that, after so many decades of threats and close calls, the Cold War ended almost overnight with barely a whisper. The world couldn't believe it. We will have a look at some of the people and circumstances that made it happen.

Finally, we will look at what happened after the Cold War ended. Every war leaves monumental changes in the lives of the people who fought in it and in the lives of those who lived through it, and the Cold war was no exception. Because there were no bombs or bullets fired by two sides at each, the usual results of war (injuries and destroyed cities) can't be seen. However, there are lots of other legacies left by the Cold War that still affect us today.

As you read through this handbook, try to put yourself into the shoes of the people involved. Can you understand why they made certain decisions? Would you have thought the same things that they thought and would you have used the same tactics that they used? As the Cold War dragged on and on and became more and more serious, would you ever have stopped and looked around to see if it was truly necessary to fight the war, or would you have kept pushing forward, determined to win?

The point of this exercise is not to judge, because it's always easy to know what should have happened when looking back and when you have all the facts. But put yourself in the shoes of the US and USSR leaders who lived back then and try to make the Cold War more real for yourself, and try to understand that something similar could happen today. Also, see if you can learn some lessons about how the stress of living through another Cold War can be avoided.

Let's start with the first section.

Chapter 1: What led up to the Cold War?

We'll start our consideration by talking about the
background of the USSR. For many years, Russia was
ruled by Tsars, or emperors. Under the rule of the Tsars, a
few people had lots of money, and the rest of the people
had little or no money. After such a long time of living day
to day without enough food to eat and without having
enough clothes to wear during the cold Russian winters,
the people of Russia wanted a change. In an important
revolution after World War One, a new type of government
was chosen: a Communist government.

Have you ever heard of a Communist government?
Communism is different from the type of government that
the United States has always used, which is called a
Federal Republic and which uses the democratic process
to make decisions. In this type of government, American
citizens vote for representatives (the candidates who they
think best represent them) and those representatives then
go to Washington DC and decide the laws that will and will

not be passed. The people of the US are happy because they feel like the federal government listens to them, and the federal government is happy because there is peace in the country and everyone is working together. In the meantime, American citizens work hard at their jobs and give part of their money to the government as taxes each year.

A communist government works a little differently.

In a communist government, the most prominent people are the members of the Communist political party, and they are the ones who make all the decisions. They vote for new leaders, they decide who will be in charge of the country, and they decide how to spend any money that the country has. They set prices for the food in the markets and decide how much to pay the farmers who grow it. The common people trust that the Communist party leaders and members will make the right decisions. And unlike many countries, where each citizen works at a job and then keeps most of the money, in a Communist country everything belongs to the Communist political party, and people live where the party tells them to, work where the party tells them to, and eat what the party tells them told to. The idea is that the rich will share with the poor and then soon there will be no rich or poor people and that everyone will have enough.

That's pretty different than the way you live, right?

Many of the poor people in Russia loved the idea of a Communist government. They thought that finally, instead of having to give their money to the Tsars and being left with nothing, that they and their families could finally have happy and productive lives. So in November of 1917, the Communist party took over the Russian government and became the new bosses. They called their new country the USSR.

Even though it had a different way of doing things, the large population of the USSR made this country an important ally during World War Two, which started a few years later. The German military, under Adolf Hitler, decided to try and invade the USSR. Hitler thought that it was a weak country and that it would easily be defeated. In fact, he said it was like an old building that just needed to be kicked a few times before it fell down on itself. Attacking the USSR seemed to fit in with Adolf Hitler's ideas for several reasons: it was a large area of land that could be used for German growth and it gave his government a chance to show that Nazi Socialism (another type of government where a lot of public things are shared by everybody) was better than Soviet Communism. So on June 22, 1941, the German army started fighting against the USSR on the Eastern Front during World War Two.

The Soviets were able to keep the Germans from taking over their country, but it wasn't an easy battle. Over ten million Soviets (Russian Communists) lost their lives fighting in the war. The country suffered immensely, especially in an economic sense. Entire towns and cities were destroyed during the war, and millions of innocent civilians were killed. Even so, despite all the harm his country had suffered, the leader of the USSR, Joseph Stalin, was able to meet with leaders from the US and Great Britain to discuss how Europe could recover from the war.

Winston Churchill, Franklin D. Roosevelt, and Joseph Stalin at the Yalta Conference in February 1945.[2]

This meeting was important because it got things started off on the right foot. It seemed like after years of fighting in Europe that everyone was going to, right from the very beginning, do things differently. They would work together and put aside their differences. Even though they spoke different languages, had different cultures, and used different forms of government, it looked like these three leaders were united by a common goal: peace in Europe.

But, the good feelings and friendships didn't last long. Soon after the Yalta Conference ended, there were deep

---

[2] Image source: http://www.history.com/photos/world-war-ii-political-leaders/photo4

concerns and mistrust which started to surface. The United States could not understand how the Soviets thought, and vice-versa. It also became clear that these two nations had different ideas of how the situation in Europe should be handled in the years after the war. For reasons we will see in the next section, The USSR was interested in making sure that its neighbors chose Communist governments just as it had done. But the United States was convinced that this was a bad idea, and they weren't about to sit back and let nation after nation become Communist.

Almost as soon as World War Two ended, the two most powerful nations in the world started to realize that they just couldn't agree with each other on a lot of genuinely salient issues. In a private report sent to the US Secretary of Defense in 1947, political advisor George Frost Keenan wrote what he thought was the best way to deal with the USSR's desires to spread their Communist ideas to other countries:

> **"In these circumstances it is clear that the main element of any United States policy toward the Soviet Union must be that of long-term, patient but firm and vigilant containment of Russian expansive tendencies."[3]**

George Frost Keenan recommended that the US government focus on "containment of Russian expansive tendencies". What did that mean? Well, if the USSR became more and more determined to convince its neighboring countries to change to Communist governments, the United States would have to begin to take small steps to make sure that didn't happen and that Communism stayed inside of the USSR; they would "contain" Communism and keep it from spreading to other countries.

Like two kids on the playground who wanted to prove which one was tougher but who didn't want to actually fight, the two countries started to push back and forth and to say some mean things to each other and about each other. As time went by, the pushing started to get harder, and the words started to get meaner.

The Cold War had begun.

[3] Quotation source: http://www.historyguide.org/europe/kennan.html

Chapter 2: Why did the Cold War happen?

After spending several years fighting World War Two and spending so much money and after suffering so many losses, why would the United States and the USSR be so quick to start another war, even if it was just a "cold" war? Why wouldn't they just agree to disagree and walk away from the fight? As we will see in this section, each side had some deep beliefs as to what they thought was going on and they were worried that if they backed down from these beliefs then something terribly bad might happen. Let's look at each side and try to understand what motivated each side to start fighting the Cold War and what kept them going for over 40 years.

The USSR: Why was the USSR so suspicious of the United States and why did they feel so motivated to spread Communism to their neighbors? Let's start with the first part of the question.

The USSR was suspicious and distrusting of the US for several reasons. First, they wondered just who the US thought they were to be bossing everyone around. It was true that American soldiers had helped to win the wars against Germany and Japan, but the Soviets felt that the American soldiers had entered the war late. In fact, it was not until June of 1944 that the first American soldiers charged into battle on the beaches of France. In the meantime, the Soviets had lost millions of soldiers and citizens while fighting against the Germans, and they thought that maybe the Americans could have helped to avoid some of the pain by helping the war effort earlier.

Also, after World War Two ended, the United States began to focus on building larger and larger nuclear weapons. The USSR felt that no nation should be putting so much emphasis on weapons in what was supposed to be a time of peace. In fact, in 1950, the National Security Council of the United States approved a national budget that increased the money going towards weapons and soldiers by 400%! The USSR was convinced that the United States did not have peaceful intentions and that maybe they needed to protect themselves from any future attacks.

The USSR was also upset with the USA because of the way Americans dealt with other countries. Officially, the

USSR felt that each country should be allowed to make its own decisions and that they shouldn't be forced one way or the other. Officially, the USA believed the same thing. But the USSR thought that the American government was constantly showing up in foreign countries around the world and telling their governments what to do. It made the Americans seem like big bullies who tried to boss around the little countries and threaten them if they didn't obey. At least, that's how the Soviets saw everything. So imagine how they felt when the US tried to stop their efforts to spread Communism to neighboring countries in Europe and Asia.

But why was the USSR so focused on spreading its government to other countries? It mainly had to do with self-preservation.

During World War Two, the USSR had been left alone to fight against the German war machine. Although they ended up eventually winning the war, millions of Soviets died in the process, and it took a long time for the country to recover. Worst of all, the attack came from Germany, a friendly country who had signed a special agreement (called a "Non-Aggression Pact") which promised that the two countries (Germany and the USSR) would never attack each other.

After that terrible experience of World War Two and fighting against Nazi Germany, the USSR knew that it couldn't survive another war like that. So the Communist Party decided to make sure that all of their neighbors were true friends who would protect them in a time of war and who would never attack them. They thought that if all the little nations around the USSR were dependent on the Communist government then they would all stick together and help each other. Plus, the USSR honestly believed that the Communist way of doing things was the best way, and they wanted others to have the benefits that they were having.

So when the USA tried to stop the USSR from spreading Communism, the Soviets saw it as a serious thing and decided that they would not back down.

The USA: Why was the USA so suspicious of the USSR and why were they opposed to the spread of Communism in Europe and Asia? Let's start with the first part of the question: Why was the USA so suspicious of the USSR?

The USA didn't like the fact that the USSR was a Communist government. That much was clear right from the start. Joseph Stalin's reputation as a brutal leader made the US wonder whether or not the Soviets were being fair to their people. There were reports of millions of people being deported to labor camps in Siberia for not supporting his way of doing things. It was also reported that during a time called "The Great Purge" in the USSR, about 1,000 people on average were killed every day for not agreeing with every little thing that the Communist party said and did.

Joseph Stalin killed many thousands of his own citizens for not agreeing with him[4]

But as much as the United States disagreed with things that were happening in the USSR, they were even more worried about the rest of the world.

---

[4] Image source: http://history1900s.about.com/od/people/ss/Stalin_6.htm

Why was the US so opposed to the spread of Communism in Europe and Asia? Well, they were worried that the human rights of many people would be violated. Do you know what "human rights" are? Human rights refer to the fact that there are certain things that everyone, no matter where they live, should be allowed to enjoy. They include having enough to eat, having a safe place to live, and not being hurt by anybody, especially by the government.

After seeing how Joseph Stalin used his Communist government to hurt millions of people, many Americans were afraid that the same thing would happen to other people if their governments became Communist. They thought that Communists force other people to think like them and to do what they say and that it takes away the rights of nations to choose for themselves how they want to live.

In fact, many in the US government were afraid of something called the "Domino Theory". This is where they thought that if one small nation in Europe or Asia became Communist then maybe other small nations would do the same thing. If all these small little nations were taken over, then pretty soon the whole world might become Communist! That was something that the United Stated did not want to happen.

So because they didn't trust each other and because they each thought that the other side wanted to hurt them, the USSR and the USA decided to keep pushing back and forth for over 40 years during the Cold War.

Chapter 3: What happened during the Cold War?

The Cold War was a time when the USSR and the USA were both trying to stop the other side from becoming too strong and when both sides were also trying to move forward with their own ideas of how the world should look. Although there were no bullets fired at each other's soldiers or bombs dropped on each other's cities, there is no doubt that these two countries did everything they could to hurt each other short of actually fighting. In this section, we will have a look at some of the tactics used during the 64 years that the Cold War was fought. We will look at four main methods used to fight the Cold War:

- **Fighting proxy wars**
- **Spreading propaganda**
- **The space race**
- **Espionage**

Let's start with the first one.

Fighting Proxy Wars. A proxy war is a war that is fought using other people's armies, kind of like playing a game of chess. But the people pulling the strings, the ones *really* in charge, see the mini-war a part of the larger war between them. All during the Cold War, the USSR and the USA used smaller wars in different parts of the world to push each other around and to try to make the other side weaker. For example, an influential proxy war fought by the USSR and USA took place in Korea.

- The Korean War lasted from June of 1950 to July of 1953, and over two million people died during it. The war was fought between North Korean soldiers (backed by Soviet weapons and money) and South Korean soldiers (backed by American money, equipment, and troops). The North Korean government wanted to make the whole area Communist, and the South Korean government wanted the country to be a democracy. Even though Soviet troops and American troops never fired a shot at each other, this war let both of them try to hurt the other side, and it let the US try to stop the spread of Communism in Asia. The war ended with the two sides agreeing to a truce and with everyone going home.

- <u>The Cuban Missile Crisis</u> was one of the scariest moments of the Cold War. Cuba had become a Communist country in 1959 after a revolution led by Fidel Castro. During the 1960s, the USSR had begun to send different types of aid to help the poor Caribbean country to feed and clothe its citizens. But in October of 1962, it was discovered that the USSR had also shipped in Soviet soldiers and nuclear weapons into Cuba. That meant that the USSR now had the ability to send their nuclear bombs to targets anywhere on the East Coast of the US, including Washington DC. President John F Kennedy had to decide how to respond, and it was decided to avoid any military action that could trigger a nuclear war. They decided to place boats all around Cuba and inspect any ships coming in, and secretly they also made a deal to remove American missiles in Turkey (a neighbor of the USSR) in exchange for the USSR removing their weapons from Cuba. The crisis was resolved, and no nuclear weapons were used. It was later said that the world had never been closer to all-out nuclear war than it was during the Cuban Missile Crisis.

- The Vietnam War was similar to the Korean War. One Asian country was in the middle of a civil war, with one part wanting to become Communist and one part wanting to remain Democratic. North Vietnam was supported by the USSR and South Vietnam by the USA. American troops went in to fight in Vietnam, and over 58,000 of them died. In the end, American troops had to retreat from the battle before it got any worse, and Vietnam, together with two neighboring countries (Laos and Cambodia) became Communist.

Spreading propaganda. Both side produced films and literature that made the other side look bad. The USSR would make posters and films about how dangerous and bloodthirsty the Americans were, and then the USA would do the same thing but talking about the Soviets. As the nuclear threat continued to grow, more movies came out talking about how easily an all-out war could happen and how terrible it would be.

The Space Race. After World War Two ended, the USA and the USSR realized the power of rockets. Rocket engines had been used by Hitler during the war to launch missiles, but now these two nations wanted to use the technology for peaceful reasons. The USSR was able to launch a satellite, called *Sputnik 1*, on October 4, 1957. This satellite was able to broadcast some basic radio signals and spent three months orbiting the earth.

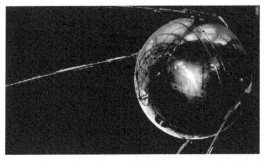

A picture of *Sputnik 1*, the satellite launched by the USSR in 1957[5]

The world was shocked at how quickly the USSR had been able to develop and launch this satellite. The USA felt like they had to catch up quickly and be the first to conquer space. After one failed attempt, the Americans were able to launch a satellite of their own four months later, the *Explorer 1*.

On April 12, 1961, the Soviets were also able to beat the USA in the next phase of the Space Race when they sent cosmonaut Yuri Gagarin into outer space in a rocket, where he then spent 108 minutes in zero gravity. Three

---

[5] Image source: http://news.blogs.cnn.com/2011/01/25/defining-a-sputnik-moment/

weeks later, on May 5, American astronaut Alan Shepard became the second man in space. Not long after that, American John Glenn became the first person ever to orbit the entire earth on February 20, 1962.

But US President John F Kennedy wanted more. After being beat by the Soviets twice, he wanted a big victory that would show the world that the USA still had what it takes and that the American tradition of exploration would continue. On September 12, 1962, he announced that before the decade of the 1960s had ended that the US would become the better space-exploration nation and that they would put men on the moon. It happened, just as Kennedy wanted, on July 20, 1969. Over 500 million people watched live on television as Neil Armstrong stepped down onto the surface of the moon. Together with Buzz Aldrin, he spent the next two hours exploring its surface.

The space race had ended, and the United States had won the final part.

Espionage. In August of 1949, the Soviet Union was able to construct and detonate a nuclear bomb. The United States, who had worked had to keep all information about its nuclear program a secret, was shocked at how fast the

Soviets had been able to build theirs. It was soon found out that there were Soviet spies in Britain and in the US stealing information and giving it to the USSR. Among them were Julius and Ethel Rosenburg, who had a public trial and were executed for their crimes.

The fact that Soviet spies had been discovered inside the American nuclear program made some people wonder where else Soviet spies might be hiding. Senator Joseph McCarthy led the charge to find and capture every spy that he could. Around the same time, the House of Representatives formed something called the "House of Un-American Activities Committee" (HUAC). A lot of attention was given to anyone, no matter who they were, who said anything that might be viewed as supporting Communism. Government officials and even reporters had to stand before cameras and promise that they were loyal to the United States.

In Hollywood, some Americans began to worry that actors, writers, and directors were secretly trying to promote Communist ideas in their films. Many famous stars were brought before different government officials and asked to promise that they weren't Communists and to give names of anyone who they thought might be.

This period in US history is called the "Red Scare" (the Communist flag was red). It was a scary time in the US because a lot of people were worried that there were spies everywhere. In fact, about ten years after the Cold War ended, it was learned that a top FBI agent named Robert Hanssen had been spying for the Soviets/Russians for 22 years. He wasn't caught until 2001!

The Cold War was unlike any war that had ever before been fought. The emphasis wasn't on domination and power; it was on control. Both sides tried to control the actions of the other side and tried to keep the enemy from getting any stronger.

Chapter 4: What was it like to be a kid during the Cold War?

An American family demonstrates how to use a bomb shelter, built in case of a nuclear war[6]

During the Cold War, there were some tense moments. For years, it would seem like nothing was going to happen and that everything was just fine, but then from one day to next (like during the Cuban Missile Crisis) it would seem as if a real war were about to break out! Imagine what it was like to be a kid growing up during that time, with the

[6] Image source: http://www.smithsonianmag.com/people-places/The-New-Hot-Item-on-the-Housing-Market-Bomb-Shelters.html

threat of war always hanging over your head, knowing that there were always thousands of missiles pointed at your city and that they could be fired at any time.

The scariest thing about living through the Cold War was not knowing what would happen the next day. As a kid, you would have seen leaders (like Presidents Nixon and Bush) trying to calm things down with the USSR, while others (like President Reagan) seemed to throw more gasoline on the fire. Also, seeing how something like the Cuban Missile Crisis brought the world so close to nuclear war would make you realize that just one or two misunderstandings could lead to the destruction of the entire planet!

In the USSR, being a kid would have been tough for all the same reasons, but there would have been a couple more things that made life even scarier. Leaders like Stalin would send whole families away to far-off areas like Siberia if they didn't agree with him or if they were part of the wrong religion. Can you imagine waking up in the middle of the night to see armed soldiers standing outside your house and demanding that you leave forever? The Communist government wanted to make itself stronger for the Cold War, and so it decided to try and eliminate any lack of unity, starting from within.

As a kid in the USSR, you would also have had to deal with the extreme poverty that many Soviets lived with. Sometimes they didn't have enough food because the government didn't give the farmers enough money. Or maybe there weren't enough jobs or the pay was too low. In the USSR, there was nothing that most people could do to change a bad situation like that, and they would simply have to deal with it.

Being a kid during the Cold War would have meant moments of being scared and wondering what would happen next.

Chapter 5: How did the Cold war end?

The Berlin Wall is torn down in 1989[7]

Most wars end with a lot of action. Soldiers use tanks and planes to conquer the capital city of a foreign nation and then force the leader to surrender or face the consequences. Pictures are taken of treaties being signed, and heroes come home to parades and awards from their governments. But when the Cold War ended, nothing like

---

[7] Image source: http://www.guardian.co.uk/politics/blog/2009/nov/09/berlin-wall-michael-white

that happened. In fact, the Cold War ended quite suddenly and in a way that no one expected- the USSR ceased to exist almost overnight. After all of the talk about military force and nuclear bombs and international relations, the whole thing ended with a few internal problems inside the USSR that collapsed the whole nation like a tent falling down after one pole is removed.

The beginning of the end for the USSR came with the appointment of Mikhail Gorbachev to head of the Communist party on March 11, 1985. Gorbachev was the first person to hold that position who had been born after the Russian revolution, and he had some different ideas as to how the government should be run. Although previous leaders like Stalin had used secrecy and violence to run the country, Gorbachev thought that the people of the USSR should be given more freedom. The Soviet economy was having some real problems during the 1980s, and Mikhail Gorbachev was convinced that the best way to fix the problems was to change the way the government ran the country and the way that it treated the people.

In 1986, Gorbachev spoke about making reforms (big changes) to the Soviet government and used a special word to describe them: *perestroika*, a word that means "restructuring". Under this new program to make the USSR more modern and more effective, more decision-making power was given to different parts of the government, persecution of different religions was stopped, and the people were given more opportunities to express their opinions, even if they went against the official position of the government.

Around this same time, a second word began to be used by Gorbachev in his speeches: *glasnost*, which meant "openness". He wanted the Soviet people to have more opportunities to share their opinions as to how their government was run. Even though the country would still be Communist, he wanted the individual Soviet to have a say in the decisions that were made and to thus take the power out of the hands of the few. Instead of hiding the problems that were in the USSR, Gorbachev wanted to bring them out into the open and to find real solutions for them.

In an important speech before the United Nations on December 7, 1988, Mikhail Gorbachev showed the world that he was serious about changing the way that things were done in the USSR, and that it wasn't just a lot of talk. He said that in the near future, he would be removing troops from several USSR satellite states in order for the locals to choose how they wanted to live and not to be afraid of upsetting the USSR and making decisions under the constant threat of punishment.

The world was shocked. The USSR, which had relied on intimidation and force for so long to keep its subjects under control, now had a leader who was making some big changes.

In the meantime, US President Ronald Reagan kept pushing for the USSR to do even more, and to move even faster. In a speech the year before, President Reagan had stood near the Berlin Wall in Germany, the wall that separated Democratic West Germany from Communist East Germany, and told the USSR to prove how progressive they were by tearing down that wall. On November 9, 1989, the wall began to be torn down, and people were allowed for the first time to leave Communist East Germany. It was the first step towards allowing the people of East Germany to decide their own future.

Other governments soon did the same. Before the year 1989 ended, four Soviet states (Bulgaria, Czechoslovakia, Lithuania, and Romania) would use their new freedoms to take steps towards changing their governments and to become independent of the USSR. In December, Mikhail

Gorbachev met with US President George H.W. Bush in Malta, and they released a statement together saying the Cold War might be coming to an end. Things were getting interesting.

During 1990, things started to move even more quickly. Six more countries took steps to become independent from the USSR (Yugoslavia, Poland, Estonia, Slovenia, Latvia, and Azerbaijan), and the two halves of Germany were officially reunited with one democratic government, one currency, and one economy.

In the meantime, a lot of events were happening in the central USSR government. Mikhail Gorbachev had an important meeting with President Bush in Washington DC, where it was decided that both countries would stop producing chemical weapons, thus just about bringing the decades-long arms race to a close. Although a lot of good things were happening in the USSR, not everyone was thrilled to see so many of the satellite countries choosing independence. In fact, not even Gorbachev himself had expected that to happen. Some within the Soviet government thought that he was doing well, but others thought that the process of reforming was talking too long as could go better. One public rival was a politician who had once been part of Gorbachev's government; his name was Boris Yeltsin.

During an attempted coup (overthrow) of the government in August of 1991, it was Boris Yeltsin who climbed on top of a tank and told everyone how wrong it was to use violence to make political decisions.

Russian President Boris Yeltsin (holding a few sheets of paper) standing in top of a tank during an attempted coup in 1991[8]

He was hailed as a hero for helping to stop the coup, but by then Mikhail Gorbachev had lost the respect of a lot of the Soviet people. Boris Yeltsin, who by this time had been elected president of Russia, declared all Communist

[8] Image source: http://thelede.blogs.nytimes.com/2007/04/23/defining-boris-yeltsin/

governments illegal in Russia, and on December 25 Mikhail Gorbachev resigned from his position as leader of the USSR and the Soviet Union thus ceased to exist, literally overnight. The Russian Federation took its seat in the UN.

The Cold War had finally ended after more than four decades of fighting, and it did so with a whisper and hardly any violence.

Chapter 6: What happened after the Cold War?

The Cold War lasted for over 40 years. Altogether, it cost the US government over $8 trillion dollars to fight, and over 100,000 American lives were lost in fighting the proxy wars (mainly in Korea and Vietnam). But the Cold War changed the face of the world and the course of history in many ways.

First, the United States was left as the only superpower. This means that only the United States currently has the strength to give an opinion on how things should be done in any spot on the globe. Only the US has enough money, political influence, and military power to back up whatever it says with action. In other words, a lot of world events since 1991, including some of the major wars that were fought, may not have happened if the USSR was still around to challenge the US and its actions.

Second, a valuable lesson was learned during the Cold War about an emotion called "paranoia". Paranoia means being afraid of something without genuinely having a good reason to be. During the investigations by Senator Joe McCarthy and the House of Un-American Activities Committee (during the "Red scare"), many Americans were afraid that there was some sort of large scale Soviet invasion happening. They began to accuse their coworkers and neighbors of being spies, and they were constantly afraid that something terrible might happen. That's called paranoia.

Well, since the fall of the Soviet Union, the United States has had other enemies, among them religious extremists from certain Middle Eastern countries. But overall, most Americans have been able to fight against the paranoia and have not given in to their fears and started to accuse their neighbors and coworkers of Middle Eastern descent of being spies or terrorists. The lesson of the Red Scare has been learned, and instead all Americans, no matter their descent, focus on the real enemy and don't fight among themselves like before.

A third result of the Cold War was that the world saw how much could be accomplished by just one politician. Mikhail Gorbachev was almost single-handedly able to bring an end to the aggressive tactics of the Soviet Union and to help the world avoid a third world war. Of course, his fellow Soviets and his government supported him, but could you imagine what things could have been like if he had never had the courage in the first place to stand up and say "Maybe we should try something a little different this time"? The world might still be in the middle of the Cold War, or worse yet, things may have evolved into another world war! Although a political leader is just one person, Mikhail Gorbachev showed how much can be accomplished when one has courage and a clear vision of the future.

Nowadays, the Russian Federation is a country that allows its citizens to work at the job of their choice and to spend their money as they want. Russia is a member of the international community and is no longer known for being violent with anybody.

But that doesn't mean that everybody is perfectly happy with every little detail of how the Cold War ended. As you may recall, there was a time when the USSR and the USA were racing to see who could build the biggest and best weapons. There were missiles, nuclear bombs, and chemical weapons produced in Soviet laboratories all across the USSR. When the Soviet Union was dissolved, there was a time when all the power and paperwork was being transferred from one government to the other, and a lot of things kind of got lost in all the transition. Although there are no confirmed reports of missing nuclear weapons, nuclear materials, or chemical weapons, a lot of experts are afraid that some underpaid scientists may have stolen certain weapons with plans to sell them later on to the highest bidder. The US government has been able to confirm that it has stopped hundreds of deals involving terrorist groups trying to buy older Soviet weapons.

Today, the world is at relative peace. Major wars involving large nations don't happen too often, and most government leaders are working hard to keep it that way. Using the examples from the Cold War, they are trying to promote good communication with all other countries and trying to avoid threats and secrets that could lead to another Cold War.

Conclusion

Wow, what a fascinating handbook this has been! We have been able to learn so much about the Cold War, and how it completely shaped many of the major events of the twentieth century and beyond. Let's have a quick review of some of the main points that we have learned.

The first section talked about what led up to the Cold War. We had a look at how the USSR was formed. After a revolution in 1917, the Communist political party took control of the government and began to make sure that everyone was going to support them. After World War Two, the Soviet Union (the organization made up of Russia and several other Communist countries) started to view the United States as an enemy. Even though the USSR and the USA had been allies during World War Two, all of that changed once the last shot of the war was fired. They quickly began to race to see who would be the strongest and the most powerful. Both sides had a clear idea of how the world should be run, and they couldn't seem to agree with each other or find any room to compromise. When President Truman decided that "containing" the Soviets was the best idea, it was clear that a Cold War was about to begin.

The next section focused on the "why", as in, "why did the Cold War happen"? Why did the two countries start to view each other as enemies and what were their motivations for trying to stop the other side from getting stronger? Although there were a lot of factors, the main idea had to do with Russia's desire to protect itself from further attack and to help other countries by teaching them about Communism. The United States, for their part, saw the USSR's attempts to spread Communism as one country trying to take over the world. Some leaders like Stalin and his harsh treatment of ordinary citizens gave Communism a bad reputation, and the US was determined to keep it from spreading to any other countries.

Then we took a closer look at what actually happened during the Cold War. We saw the four different tools each side used to try to make themselves stronger and the other guy weaker. The four tactics included:

- **Fighting proxy wars**. The USSR and USA faced off against each other in different countries in order to keep the other side from getting stronger. They faced off in Korea, Cuba, and Vietnam, and in each instance the world watched and wondered if it would get more serious. Especially during the

Cuban Missile Crisis, some high-level politicians thought that a nuclear war was about to start.

- **Spreading propaganda.** Both sides tried to use books, movies, and speeches to make themselves look better and the other side look worse. The propaganda worked sometimes, but it also led to many Americans being terrified of what might happen if a nuclear war were to break out.

- **The space race.** Each side wanted to show that their government was the strongest and that their scientists were the best. So beginning in the 1950s and lasting until 1969, both sides competed to be the first to send a satellite into space, to send a man into outer space in a rocket ship, to have him orbit the earth, and then to send a man to the moon. Although the Soviets won the first few rounds of the battle, President John F Kennedy gave a lot of attention to the US space program and, thanks to his efforts and the work of many scientists, two Americans landed on the moon on July 20, 1969.

- **Espionage.** Both the USSR and the USA wanted to learn what the other side was doing, so they used threats, money, and spies to get information from each other's governments. When a few Soviet spies were caught in the United States, it started a sort of panic where everyone started to think that there were many spies and that their friends and neighbors might be Soviet secret agents working for the enemy. This panic was known as the "Red Scare".

It was fascinating to have a first row seat and see how each of these methods worked and how they influenced daily life in each of the countries involved.

Then we saw what it was like to be a kid back then. What do you think it was like to grow up knowing that a huge country out there wanted to destroy the place where you lived? How would it feel to know that someone was spreading lies about you and your family to win an election or to score a political point? Would you have felt safe knowing that there were thousands of missiles aimed at your country, ready to be fired at a moment's notice? We saw that no matter where you lived, whether it was in the USA or in the USSR, you would probably have been pretty scared at certain moments, like during bomb drills or during the Cuban Missile Crisis. Can you ask your parents or some other adult what it was like to be alive back then?

The next section showed us how the Cold War finally came to an end. You may be surprised to find out that, after so many decades of threats and close calls, the Cold War ended almost overnight with a whisper. As we saw, the internal problems in the USSR led to the Communist party choosing a new leader, Mikhail Gorbachev. Gorbachev tried to fix the problems in his country by changing the way the Soviet government operated, and the freedom that it gave to the different Communist countries led to their declaring their independence and the Soviet Union being disbanded in 1991. The world couldn't believe it: the Cold war had ended with barely a whisper.

Finally, we looked at what happened after the Cold War ended. Every war leaves huge changes in the lives of the people who fought in it and who lived through it, and the Cold war was no different. Because there were no bombs or bullets fired by the two sides at each other, the usual results of war (injuries and destroyed cities) can't be seen. However, there are lots of other legacies left by the Cold War that still affect us today. The US is the only superpower still around, and Russia is a much different country today than it was back then. The world's leaders have learned a lot of good lessons about the power of communication and bravery, and it has helped to maintain the peace in recent years.

The Cold War was a unique time in US history. It was a time when many people thought that their enemy could be anywhere and that a nuclear war might break out at any moment. However, thanks to the actions of several brave leaders who were willing to try new things and to make tough choices, there was no World War Three and no nuclear bombs were ever dropped.

Were you able to put yourself into the shoes of the people involved? Could you understand why they made the decisions they made? In the heat of the moment, politicians and everyday people can sometimes think and do some pretty crazy things. Do you think that you would have supported Stalin as he used violence to intimidate all rivals, or would you have been more like Mikhail Gorbachev who encouraged communication and openness?

The Cold War ended back in 1991, but there are still enemies of the United States who would try to use their power and influence to boss other people around. Will there be another Cold war in the future? If everyone learns from the examples of leaders like President Reagan, Mikhail Gorbachev, President Bush, and Boris Yeltsin, then maybe another dangerous conflict like this one can be avoided.

Today, the Russian Federation works with the United
Nations to promote world peace[9]

---

[9] Image source: http://www.rferl.org/content/russia-proposes-un-resolution-syria-without-sancions/24641349.html

Made in the USA
Las Vegas, NV
01 March 2023